Food for Life

OCEANS

KATE RIGGS

Published by Creative Education
P.O. Box 227, Mankato, Minnesota 56002
Creative Education is an imprint of The Creative Company
www.thecreativecompany.us

Design and production by Liddy Walseth
Art direction by Rita Marshall
Printed in the United States of America

Photographs by Getty Images (Pete Atkinson, Fred Bavendam, Aldo Brando,
Bill Curtsinger, David Doubilet, Jeff Foott, David Nardini, Chris Newbert,
Paul Nicklen, Flip Nicklin, Silvia Otte, DR & TL Schrichte, Thayer Syme,
Darryl Torckler, D. P. Wilson/FLPA, Art Wolfe, Norbert Wu),
Minden Pictures (Mike Parry)

Library of Congress Cataloging-in-Publication Data
Riggs, Kate.
Oceans / by Kate Riggs.
p. cm. — (Food for life)
Includes index.
Summary: A fundamental look at a common food chain in the ocean, starting
with the microscopic plankton, ending with the killer whale, and introducing
various animals in between.
ISBN 978-1-58341-828-4
1. Marine ecology—Juvenile literature. 2. Food chains (Ecology)—
Juvenile literature.
I. Title. II. Series.

QH541.5.S3R54 2010
577.7'16—dc22 2009004781

First Edition
2 4 6 8 9 7 5 3 1

Food for Life

OCEANS

KATE RIGGS

A GREEN BOOK

A food chain shows what living things in an area eat. Plants are the first link on a food chain. Animals that eat plants or other animals make up the rest of the links.

An ocean is a large body of water. The water in an ocean is salty. People cannot drink saltwater. But a lot of plants and animals can live in it.

CORAL REEFS LOOK

BUT THEY ARE MADE

LIKE COLORFUL ROCKS,
FROM THE BODIES OF _CORAL_.

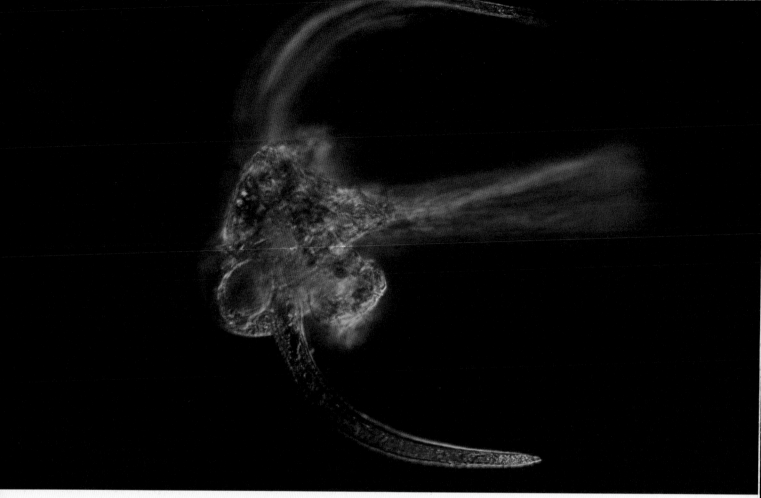

Tiny plants called plankton live in the ocean. Plankton do not grow in the ground like most plants. They float near the top of the water. They do not have roots that hold them in one place.

Sardines eat plankton. The small, silvery fish live near _coasts_. Sardines swim in big groups called schools. A school of sardines can eat a lot of plankton!

LEATHERBACK SEA TURTLES
THEIR FAVORITE

ARE FAST SWIMMERS.
FOOD IS THE BOX JELLYFISH.

A much bigger fish called a salmon eats sardines. It looks for a school of sardines. Then it uses its sharp teeth to grab as many sardines as it can. It swallows the smaller fish whole.

Sea lions are smart ocean animals that eat salmon. A sea lion has wide flippers that help it swim. It swims to where it knows salmon will be. **Then it eats a big meal.**

A sea lion can become a meal for another _predator_. The black-and-white killer whale likes to eat sea lions. Killer whales team up to hunt for _prey_.

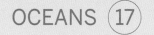

THE SMART DOLPHIN EATS

DOLPHINS MIGHT BE

SMALL FISH AND SQUID.
EATEN BY LARGER SHARKS.

All of these living things make up a food chain. The plankton floats in the ocean. The sardine eats the plankton. The salmon eats the sardine. The sea lion eats the salmon. And the killer whale eats the sea lion.

FIN WHALES ARE THE SECOND-LARGEST ANIMALS IN THE WORLD. THEY EAT PLANKTON AND SMALL FISH.

GREAT WHITE SHARKS
ARE AT THE TOP OF THE
OCEAN FOOD CHAIN. NO
ANIMAL HUNTS THEM.

Some day, the killer whale will die. Its body will break down into _nutrients_ (NOO-tree-ents). These nutrients will flow through the ocean and help plants such as the plankton grow. Then the ocean food chain will start all over again.

READ MORE ABOUT IT

Fleisher, Paul. *Ocean Food Webs*. Minneapolis: Lerner Publications, 2008.

Lynch, Emma. *Ocean Food Chains*. Chicago: Heinemann Library, 2005.

GLOSSARY

coasts—the edges of the land closest to the water

coral—small ocean animals that have hard skeletons and live in groups called colonies

nutrients—things in soil and food that help plants and animals grow strong and healthy

predator—an animal that kills and eats other animals

prey—an animal that is eaten by another animal

INDEX